Only Beth

AF504286

T Bared

Presentation by *BookLeaf Publishing*

Web: www.bookleafpub.com

E-mail: info@bookleafpub.com

ISBN: 9789357441773

First edition 2023

To my Beth.

Thank you for the dance.

ACKNOWLEDGEMENT

I can't name them and they will never read this so I shall say no more than, I am sorry!

PREFACE

I had hoped that in some small way, the writing of these poems would help me heal.
I am as yet unsure whether this was achieved or whether they simply worked to make the pain more tangible, and to keep Beth more alive to me.

The yoyo dog

In conversations about you
With my mother and her son,
My brother states I am a dog in all of this.
That I pander to you,
Crawl to you,
Beg at your feet and howl at the moon.

These aren't his exact words,
But it is what I hear,
And he is right.
He means to say that I am chasing you,
Too eager,
And losing you because of it.

He says I should be more cat.
That if I show less emotion,
You will turn to face me once more.

That like a dog
I bound to greet the very smallest of your
kindnesses,
Even after you have kicked me,
Shooed me from you
And left me hungry for days,
sometimes weeks.

My brother states I need to man up,
That the person you met, the one you liked
Is not the one I am currently being.
That to chase you for kindness
Will chase you away,
And I know that he is right.

My mother paints the truth more simply.
She says, 'You are a yoyo!'
'And that woman has a firm hold upon your
string'.

I cannot un-love you

I watched a movie once and,
Horrified by it's content learnt
That to see is to never un-see.
I can never un-see those things I saw.

I heard a tale with howling at its core,
And learned once more
That to hear is to never unhear,
I will never unhear that howl.
I only wish I could.

And like these truths
I have loved you.
Still do, in a most painful way,
And I am learning that I will never,
Can never, un-love you.
You are never going away.

I will never again unknow your face,
Unknow the sound of your laugh,
Unknow the touch of your lips against my
cheek,
I am doomed and damned forever,
To know you and to love you.

And somehow, this seems right!

Am I no longer your Freddie?

You sent a text,
Cold and hard,
No Freddie,
No Teddie,
No kiss,
Only this,
'I'm sorry!
I think it's best not to stay in contact.',
And I can't even ask you for reasons,
I can't know if you are ok,
Can't breathe.

Please!

Please woman
Get out of my head,
Stop crawling, creeping
Around my bed,
Looking to invade my dreams.

Enough already
I have seen too much,
Only felt your briefest touch,
Crave you always,
Just leave me be.

I can't sleep,
I can't close my eyes,
For fear of seeing you there,
Or seeing you not there,
Which is by far the greater fear.

Please stop the torment
You are everywhere,
In the music,
In the movement of trees,
In the taste of the stale bread I had for breakfast.

Please just let me be,
You want something,
But that something is not me,
This has been made abundantly clear,
So please!

As the sun

You have burned me up,
Eaten through my epidermis
And sucked all moisture from my soul,
Left me wizened and befuddled,
As would the sun.

You warmed me briefly,
Before turning your rays
In deadly calefaction,
To singe me, brittle and cracked,
As does the sun.

There is no shade from you
That I can find,
You scald my eyes,
Blind my mind and leave me thirstful,
As may the sun.

You shine and offer hope,
And I, stupid,
In my cold and needing place
Turn to you always, offer my face, my entirety,
As to the sun.

In Out Un On

In love with you,
In pain without,
Insane without a doubt.

Outcast from you,
Outside and cold,
Out of my mind, tormented.

Untouched by you,
Unloved it seems,
Unstable in every barely tenable way.

On time you were,
On fire was I,
On my mind, on and on every day!

Day 5

The day is only beginning
It's slow descent
Into another lonely night,
As like life,
And eventual death.

The day only starts
To ultimately end,
The time between
Passes too fast,
Or all too often inchmeal.

I'm awake and fearful,
Not knowing,
whether this will be a fast
or unbearably protracted day,
I'm guessing at both.

Too fast for me
To make use of it
In any meaningful way,
Too slow for me to elude
The so-called healing passage of time.

Healing hurts more than dying

I think,
And sleep is a refuge, to me
denied,
I pray for all my days ends,
It is 5 days since you last spoke!

Try

I am lusty,
Filled with every emotion denied by you,
Each of which now
Placed upon some poor other soul,
God protect her.

It's the song she sings,
Her hair, her effort,
She wants not me,
But I could, can, do,
But only for the want of you.

So are you to blame here?
You left me bereft,
Needing and wanting,
Hungry and dead,
This girl is not you.

She is so soft,
Hard at her core, she thinks,
Unlike you,
The reverse
I think,
But I could fall.

I can't!
She is incredible,
Unbelievable,
Unattainable,
Not for me,
And so?

I find myself looking for you.
I go back to previous haunts,
I seek you on your insta,
I imagine you will be mine and
Try not to fall for a friend in your absence.

There is no doubt

I have awoken today, sad
And missing you,
And feeling like you might call,
My heart is trying to fool me
Once more.

She thinks of you
Says my heart,
Almost as much as you think of her,
She will return, it says,
Like a promise.

She wants you
Shouts my heart,
More than she can say,
She's missing you, it cries
every single day.

She will come to you
Whispers my heart,
To be where she is supposed to be,
In our embrace,
Lying next to me.

My heart she is a liar,
Assures me of happy endings,
That's what she is about.
But, I know you will not call me,
Of this, I have no doubt.

Nothing

Nothing happens
When I do nothing,
And when I do something
Nothing good happens anyway.

So which is better?
Do something?
Do nothing?
Do away with the concept of doing?

Do I?
Do you?
Do we?
I don't think so!

So mad at you for leaving me like this,
So sad that we lost that one crucial stage,
I did nothing
So nothing has happened.
I should have done something!
Because now everything has changed.

Out out!

I decided,
I needed,
Human contact,
A connection.
I went out out!

Hit a pub,
Then hit a club,
Met a girl,
Then hit the floor.
Man, I was out out!

Drank a little,
Drank a lot,
Drank way too much.
I lost the girl.
I was so very out out!

Got kicked out,
Got a little lost,
Then got depressed.
Got very stressed.
I don't think I much like going out out.

And now it's focus blurred

My wife,
Because by law
And in name,
She is still this,
Called me yesterday.

Out of the blue,
Her name in my phone,
My heart in my throat,
Still drunk from last night,
And still feeling a need for connection.

I thought first to avoid.
Ignore and flee,
It's not time enough yet.
But biting the bullet, and feeling sorry for
myself,
I called her.

She wept,
Just wanting to hear my voice,
Nothing really to say,
So troubled, so sad,
I wept along with her.

I've had my resolve,
These past 2 months
That my decision is made,
Is sound,
Is correct.

But hearing her voice,
Her pain,
Her despair,
I wanted to hold her,
Do almost anything to comfort.

And without you nearby,
To think fondly of,
I am left with far too much time,
Time to consider her pain,
Time to understand what I have done.

I could hate myself more,
Without the wanting of you I could truly despise myself,
For I have broken this girl,
Shattered her dreams,
And upended her life.

And I'm so terribly sad,
So horribly sad for her loss,
But it doesn't feel like mine,
Because my loss is with you,
Sitting like a jewel in your crown.

That realisation,
It makes me feel shallow,
Uncaring and cold,
I never saw myself this way,
And I wonder what I have become.

I didn't leave just to be with you Beth,
I have said it one hundred times,
But I wonder now,
Is this the truth or
Was it me I was trying to convince?

In truth it is this,
I still love her, sincerely,
I know this by how I hurt at her hurt,
But I could never go back there,
As I would always be thinking of you.

Play on

I had started to forget you!
But then I looked once again
For the video that I love of you,
And it is gone.

I can only imagine
You have removed it,
Because you know that I watch it,
And because you wish me not to.

I loved that video!
It was all you,
You played so tragically beautiful,
And moved so right.

It's ok though,
I have it memorised,
Have it etched into my brain,
The way you tilt your head.

The tapping of your foot,
The way you were obviously irked
By the sudden end of the song,
When you could have happily played on.

I messaged

I was drunk,
And I messaged,
And I'm sorry.
I know you asked me not to,
I didn't want to,
But only because you didn't want me to.

In truth,
I really wanted to,
Truly needed to.
But I was drunk,
I shouldn't have,
And that was bad.

I asked for closure,
Asked what I've done,
Demanded answers.
Not sure I had the right,
Not sure it was even safe,
Not good, I'm sorry.

I told you how I hurt,
How I cannot stop!
How I think of you always.
I should have said nothing,

Should have shut up,
I should have deleted your number.

I cried as I wrote it,
You don't know that fact,
You'll never know that fact.
I cried when I re-read it,
I had accused you for my pain,
I had no right to do that.

I wrote another,
Saying sorry,
Saying it was the last.
I meant it,
I truly meant it,
I know I have to stop!

Then you responded,
So unlike you!
I was surprised.
You wrote so kindly,
You offered me closure,
But sadly, I only feel hope.

I have re-read your message

I have re-read your last message,
Over and over,
Scoured it relentlessly.
Trying to find all the tiny nuances,
The possible hidden meanings,
The truth among your words.

It seems to me the truth is this,
You are either being kind,
Letting me off easy.
Or that you want me, desire me,
But that our shared desire will burn us up,
Kill us all!

If there were only you and I,
I would be ready for the flames.

Tread lightly

I wish I could
Tread lightly,
Tiptoe through this life,
Make less impact,
Leave less mess.
Maybe tread lightly enough,
To tiptoe into your dreams,
Unperceived by any other,
Not even by you,
And without causing additional calamity.

Untitled

25

It seems true to me
That a good love always ends with pain.
It is inevitable if you think about it.
One either leaves or dies,
The survivor must bear the weight.
In hindsight love is a cruelty regardless.

Sick & Twisted

I want only what is best for you,
I swear this is the truth,
And in my mind
And in my heart,
I believe that this is me.

I feel that I can love you,
Like no other person can,
That I can cherish
And adore you more,
Than you even knew was possible.

I write our story like a fiction,
Full of angst and full of passion,
I write our future like a drama
All angles with soft edges,
Yet there is no hope for a future here.

Your future is with him,
The man you married some years past,
And I have to establish ways to erase him
For my fiction to ever work,
And for this I am despicable!

For I want only the best for you,
And the thoughts I have of him
Are dark at their edges,
Bleeding masses of unpleasantness,
That reek of an inner sickness.

He may well be what is best for you,
I've not given that much thought,
For to do so would be to quit us,
I'm not ready,
I cannot do it!

But I really do want only good for you,
And the things that I think of him,
The reasons he might leave
Or be extracted from you,
Evil all of them!

The horrors he would have to accomplish!
The things he would have to say!
The things that would have to happen,
All of these things horrendous!
I try to avoid these broodings.

I want only what is best for you,
And in these thoughts, I can plainly see
I am not what's best for you,
Because I have these thoughts unbidden,
And in some sick and twisted way, I want them.

Bored no more

Bored,
On a train,
Tired from the day,
Another filled with missing you.

Tired,
Still far to go,
I check my phone,
Then check my other, I have two.

Your name!
A request!
Confusing at best,
After shutting us down so completely.

Heart,
Stomach,
Mind,
All leaping about.

LinkedIn,
Like before,
Yet this time it means
So much more.

Disentomb,
From beneath ground,
Connection resumed,
I look for the request.

Gone!
No longer there,
You changed your mind?
I barely care.

Because you!
You wanted to connect,
You thought of me,
You took a risk.

Good!
I am glad you changed your mind,
Yours is a dangerous game,
Mine, not so much for me.

LinkedIn,
I look for you there,
But you are gone, utterly gone,
And now I am scared.

My mind,
Turns to why,
And I see clearly, you caught!
Him angry and deleting your profile.

Nothing,
My mind can think of nothing,
No other explanation,
I am scared!

Understanding,
Of what we or I alone maybe,
Have done here,
I hope aloud for your safety.

Nothing,
There is nothing I can do!
No one I can ask,
No way to know if you are ok.

Stop!
That is all that I can do,
To protect you both
I must stop.

Here

So, this is all that's left,
This place
And my memories.
No new memories can be made,
I cannot let that happen.

This is now,
The only place that I can find you,
The only place I know to be safe
Where I can assure,
You both remain unharmed.

I love you!
That's what I really want to say,
I love you more than I can put in this book,
More than I have ever told,
And I want you!

And all the words in the world,
All the secret viewings of your picture,
All the secret messages,
All my dreams of us together,
All come down to this.

So here is my last refuge,
Safety assured,
So very few shall read these pages,
I shall write it only here,
I love you.

88 days, 16 hours, 24 minutes and 34 seconds

88 days, 16 hours, 24 minutes and 34 seconds
approximately
Since I very first saw you,
I never believed in love at first sight,
But there you were,
And you were everything!

And I'm sorry,
Because I cannot end this book well.
There are no good words in my head,
To say goodbye to you Beth,
And my fingers would refuse to type them
anyway.

Freddie 21/01/23 - 11:22am